Movements in Art **GOTHIC ART**

Movements in Art GOTHIC ART

JESSICA GUNDERSON

CREATIVE EDUCATION

Published by Creative Education
P.O. Box 227, Mankato, Minnesota 56002
Creative Education is an imprint of The Creative Company.

Design and production by Blue Design (www.bluedes.com)
Art direction by Rita Marshall
Printed in the United States of America

Photographs by Alamy (Arco Images, V&A images, Visual Arts Library (London)), Art Resource (German School, Scala), The Bridgeman Art Library (American School (19th century), Luis Borrassa, Duccio di Buoninsegna, Ambrogio Lorenzetti), Corbis (Elio Ciol, Terry W. Eggers, Adam Woolfitt), Getty Images (Altrendo Travel, David A. Barnes, Nicholas Bataille, Bruno De Hogues, French School, Giotto di Bondone, Hulton Archive, Imagno, Italian School, Simone Martini, Tommaso Masaccio, Master Bertram of Minden, Master Mateo, Martin Moos, Panoramic Images, Antoine Rivalz, Anthony Frederick Augustus Sandys, Time & Life Pictures)

Library of Congress Cataloging-in-Publication Data

Gunderson, Jessica.
Gothic art / by Jessica Gunderson.
p. cm. — (Movements in art)
Includes index.
ISBN 978-1-58341-610-5
1. Art, Gothic—Juvenile literature. 2. Architecture, Gothic—Juvenile literature. I. Title. II. Series.

N6310.G86 2008
709.02'2—dc22   2007018952

9 8 7 6 5 4 3 2

Cover: Meeting at the Golden Gate and the Presentation in the Temple by
    Master Bertram of Minden (1400–10)
Page 2: Interior of the Sainte-Chapelle
Pages 4–5: The Annunciation, detail of the angel Gabriel by Giotto (c. 1305)

Gothic Art

The history of the world can be told through accounts of great battles, the lives of kings and queens, and the discoveries and inventions of scientists and explorers. But the history of the way people think and feel about themselves and the world is told through art. From paintings of the hunt in prehistoric caves, to sacred art in the Middle Ages, to the abstract forms of the 20th century, movements in art are the expression of a culture. Sometimes that expression is so powerful and compelling that it reaches through time to carry its message to another generation.

Gothic art flourished toward the end of the Middle Ages. Heavily focused on religious subjects and expressive of people's faith in the Catholic Church, Gothic artists created some of the most exquisite cathedrals, such as the Notre-Dame de Paris.

With all their intricate detail, which sometimes included individual statues of prophets (left), most Gothic cathedrals took hundreds of years to complete. In fact, work continues today on the Milan Cathedral (opposite) in Italy, which was begun in 1386.

In villages across Europe from Poland to France, cathedral spires scrape the clouds, rising high above the houses and people below to dominate the landscape with their grandeur. Many of these cathedrals were built in the Gothic age, the period from A.D. 1150 to 1400, a time of faith and spiritual devotion. Inside the cathedrals, stained-glass windows color the walls, magnificent altarpieces tell biblical stories, and statues and sculptures depict religious figures and saints, all intended to instruct, awe, and inspire spiritual loyalty in those who entered these majestic structures.

THE RISE OF GOTHIC ART

Life in Europe in the Middle Ages—the period from A.D. 500 to 1450—was filled with religious celebration, courtly love, and prosperity. **Medieval** society was organized according to feudalism, a system in which the king owned all the land in a country, and he gave land grants to wealthy lords in return for their service in the military. The lords, in turn, gave their protection to the **peasants** who worked their land. Though many people in the Middle Ages still lived in rural areas, by the 12th century, towns centralized around the property of lords were springing up all over Europe. Stone walls enclosed the towns' streets, wells, markets, shops, and churches, and within the walls, a feeling of community grew.

Abbot Suger's innovative designs for the church of Saint-Denis were inspired by his readings of early Christian philosophers, which led him to incorporate as much light as possible into the building through the use of stained glass and vaulted ceilings.

The artisans and tradespeople of the towns often formed guilds, or associations, that were vital to a community's sense of spirit and unity. Guildsmen organized town celebrations and meetings and looked after townspeople in times of trouble. Peddlers traveled from town to town trading goods, and as trade increased between the villages, ideas about art and culture spread.

Although the 12th century was a time of growth and prosperity, it was also a time of danger, **famine**, and disease. Homes, which ranged from stone houses to wood-and-thatch dwellings, were built close together, and because open flames were used for cooking and heating, houses caught fire easily. Fires leaped rapidly from building to building, often destroying entire villages. Disease also spread quickly in the close-knit towns. Populations rose and fell. When the population of Europe reached a height of nearly 100 million in the mid-14th century, food became scarce, and many people suffered from hunger.

During these uncertain times, many people turned to the Catholic Church for comfort and sanctuary. Because most medieval people were illiterate, the word of God was spread through images on altarpieces (paintings or sculptures placed above and behind an altar), statues, and devotional figures within the churches. But churches were not always accessible to the common people. Solemnity and solitude among the monks and priests was encouraged, and many abbeys and cathedrals were located in rural, secluded areas.

That changed in the 1130s, when Abbot Suger (1081–1151) of the monastery of Saint-Denis in the region of Île-de-France near Paris decided to rebuild the abbey church in order to make Saint-Denis a religious center of France. As a lover of architecture, Abbot Suger had taken careful note of the designs of

One of the best-known Gothic cathedrals in the world, the Notre-Dame de Paris features single-arch flying buttresses that support the eastern end of the cathedral. The use of flying buttresses enabled taller, thinner-walled cathedrals to be built.

THE CRUSADES

The Crusades were a series of military campaigns waged by European Christians with the goal of recapturing the Holy Land from the Muslims who controlled it. For hundreds of years, Europeans had been traveling to Jerusalem, a city that was sacred to them as the birthplace of Christianity, but when the Muslim Turks took over the city in 1071, the new rulers did not

welcome Christian visitors. In 1095, Pope Urban II urged Christians to fight for the Holy Land, and the Crusades began. From 1095 to 1291, seven Crusades were fought before the Muslims finally secured the land as their own. Through the course of the wars, many lives were lost, but the Crusades also introduced Europeans to a new culture and opened trade between Europe and the Mediterranean states.

buildings in other parts of the continent on his many travels. He incorporated many elements of these designs, such as sculpted, arched doorways, called portals, and decorated fronts and sides, when remodeling the Saint-Denis church. He also hired stoneworkers and sculptors from the Saint-Denis area as well as from other regions of France, which helped to set the completed church apart from surrounding churches and cathedrals.

One of the aspects that made Saint-Denis innovative and exceptional was Suger's quest for light within the church. Suger believed that light was of holy origin and was the link between spirit and body and heaven and earth, and he wished to dispel the darkness common in earlier **Romanesque** structures by installing windows that would filter sunlight into the church. The development of the ribbed vault, a series of intersecting arches that support the roof of a building, allowed for the placement of more windows than in earlier buildings, which used thick, solid vaults that supported thick, solid walls. Suger's design for Saint-Denis was one of the first major buildings to use the ribbed vault. With the completion of the cathedral at Saint-Denis, a new style of architecture known as French Gothic and characterized by ribbed vaults, **flying buttresses**, and a focus on interior light soon spread throughout the region and into neighboring countries.

At the same time as Gothic architecture was flourishing in France, the Christian Crusades—religious wars fought in Israel in the 11th, 12th, and 13th centuries—were bringing Western Europe into contact with other cultures of the world, especially those of the **Byzantine Empire** and **Islamic** Arabia. In addition to new mathematical systems, including algebra, these cultures introduced Europeans to the ideas of important Classical Greek

THE HUNDRED YEARS' WAR

The Hundred Years' War was a series of armed conflicts between France and England from 1337 to 1453. The war resulted from disputes between the ruling families of France and England over territories in France. Each family claimed reign over the French

wine-producing region of Gascony, among others, and what began as small skirmishes in Gascony grew into a lengthy war. The war saw the use of new weapons, such as the cannon and longbow, and the employment of professional armies rather than peasant soldiers. Due to the devastation and expense of the war, cathedral building in France slowed, bringing about the end of Gothic architecture in many areas of the country.

and Roman **philosophers**, such as Aristotle, who promoted scholastic, rational reasoning rather than faith-based thinking. This new rational thought influenced the arts significantly. While previous styles of religious art and architecture, namely the Romanesque, dwelt on darkness, fear, and solemnity, the heightened interest in scholastic thinking during the Gothic period promoted a more rational look at religion's function in the world. Beauty in nature and art went from being seen as a temptation from the devil to being looked upon as a logical creation of God. Builders during this time sought to reflect a divinely ordered universe in the architecture and sculpture of their churches. Rather than frighten, they thought cathedrals should illuminate the love of God for God's world.

Stimulated by new developments in architecture and the concentration of people within towns, the great age of cathedral building began. Between the years 1250 and 1400, more than 500 large churches and cathedrals sprang up in towns throughout Europe. The ribbed vault allowed for heightened ceilings, spires, and towers, and the cathedrals reached toward heaven in awe-inspiring grandeur. Architects filled the cathedrals with light by installing many small windows next to each other, most of which were made of stained glass. Inside the cathedrals, spears of colored light shifted with the changing sun.

The construction of a cathedral often took more than a century to complete. Hundreds of workers were employed to build a single structure. Wagons and mules carried building materials, such as stone and wood, for miles. A master builder was in charge of executing the design, but because construction spanned generations, often more than one master builder worked

Medieval tapestries were not restricted to sacred subjects. They were also made to recount the legends of knights, the activities of nobles, and scenes of surrounding landscapes. The art of the tapestry flourished under the hands of French weavers during the Middle Ages.

on a cathedral. Both during and after their construction, cathedrals were the focus of the towns, and church officials often raised the taxes of the peasants and townspeople in order to fund the building of the cathedrals.

Inside Gothic cathedrals, religious art informed and inspired worshipers. During the Middle Ages, most art was made for the purpose of religious instruction, and very little secular, or nonreligious, art flourished. Narrative art relating biblical stories emerged as **tapestries**, altarpieces, sculptures, **frescoes**, and stained-glass windows told stories of God and Jesus Christ, prophets and saints, and the Virgin Mary. Illuminated manuscripts—prayer books and religious manuscripts that were decorated with borders and illustrations—were created in abundance for the wealthy during the Gothic period.

Whereas earlier religious art was made up of **symbols**, Gothic art relied upon the portrayal of realistic human figures to express the narrative. Much Gothic art was characterized by extreme emotions, such as deep suffering or heightened ecstasy in the presence of God. The humanistic and naturalistic aspects of Gothic works of art were made possible by artists' increased understanding of perspective—the proportions of objects and their surroundings. Artists began placing their figures within architectural and natural settings, increasing the realism of the figures, and making facial features more pronounced and accurate. Even though painters and sculptors were becoming more involved in the concepts behind their art, they were considered skilled craftsmen who worked with their hands rather than their minds and were not held in great esteem. For this reason, many great Gothic artists remain **anonymous** today.

The biggest tapestry in the world is housed in the Castle of Angers in the French province of Anjou. Created by weaver Nicholas Bataille between 1373 and 1387, the 459-foot (140 m) tapestry tells the biblical story of the apocalypse with scenes such as "St. John Eating the Book."

Many master Gothic artisans used lodge books to illustrate concepts and techniques when teaching apprentices and assistants about their craft. Villard de Honnecourt faithfully recorded architectural techniques in the pages of his lodge book.

ARTISTS OF THE GOTHIC PERIOD

Villard de Honnecourt (c. 1225–50), a French architect and master mason, or stoneworker, who is believed to have worked on the designs of cathedrals in the towns of Reims and Laon, is today valued more for his sketchbook than for his role in building cathedrals. As a master mason, Honnecourt traveled widely in search of work, and as he traveled, he collected an array of ideas from French regions, from Switzerland, and from as far away as Hungary. He filled his sketchbook with drawings of figures from life and of the architecture of the churches and cathedrals he came across, and then later compiled his drawings and ideas into a text that he may have used to teach students of architecture.

Of this book, 33 **parchment** leaves containing more than 250 drawings exist today. In addition to gathering information from other regions to bring back to his native Picardy, France, Honnecourt helped spread the artistic ideas of Picardy to other parts of the continent, contributing to the growth of Gothic art and architecture in Europe.

Besides gathering and spreading others' ideas, Honnecourt also developed some unique innovations of his own. His drawings provide instruction on how to use geometric shapes to form figures—such as the human head and body—as well as how to use geometry to make larger images, a technique that various artists, from architects to sculptors to fresco painters, employed both during the Gothic period and today.

Although Gothic ideas were born in France, by the mid-13th century, they had spread to other areas of Europe, mostly by way of small objects, such as devotional figures and small statues made in Paris and circulated to other French regions and beyond. Italy was an important artistic center that felt the

French Gothic influence, and there Italian sculptors Nicola Pisano (c. 1220–84) and his son Giovanni Pisano (c. 1250–1314) combined French Gothic flavors with Classical Roman and Greek styles, which were characterized by the use of simple, straight lines and freestanding statues. This combination of French Gothic and Classical styles became one of the defining characteristics of the Italian Gothic style.

Nicola Pisano was born in southern Italy, where Classical styles were being revived, but he spent much of his artistic career as a hired sculptor in Pisa and Siena in central Italy.

Gothic architects sometimes went as far back as ancient Greece to gather inspiration for their work, such as these carved Corinthian column capitals found on the Chartres Cathedral. What sets these apart from Classical columns, though, are the distinctly medieval images of knights and dragons.

His sculpture of the birth of Jesus Christ, entitled *Nativity* (1260), on a pulpit in the Pisa Baptistery (the chamber where baptisms were held) reflects both Classical trends in its realistic figures and Gothic ideas in its depiction of the draped cloths upon the figures. Nicola brought an empathetic humanity into his religious figures, a concept that many sculptors in later years would repeat.

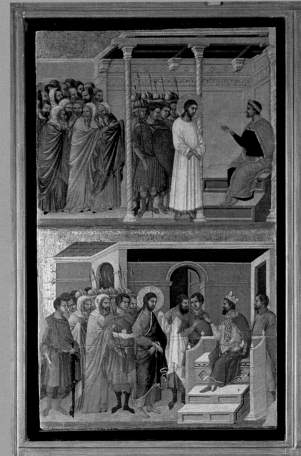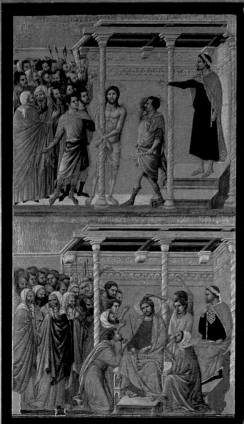

Nicola's son Giovanni assisted his father with his later projects, but by the end of the 13th century, Giovanni had emerged as an individual artist with his own style and technique, though his father's influence was still evident in his work. Like his father, Giovanni also made a sculpture called *Nativity* (1302–10) on a pulpit in the Pisa Cathedral, but unlike his father's pulpit, upon which the figures are crowded together, Giovanni's sculpture depicts the figures as spaced apart, putting the focus on the space and shadows that surround them rather than on only the figures themselves.

The Gothic style of Giovanni Pisano had a great influence on prominent Italian painter Duccio di Buoninsegna (c. 1255–1319), who was working in Siena at the same time as Giovanni. In his magnificent work *Maestà Altarpiece* (1308–11), painted for the Siena Cathedral, Duccio used the Gothic naturalism that he had learned from viewing Giovanni's work to portray his figures as realistic and three-dimensional. The infant Jesus Christ is especially lifelike, and the angels and saints who surround Mary and Jesus wear various, individual expressions upon their faces. Duccio painted each of the figures with long **silhouettes**, bringing to them an elegance that was characteristic of Gothic art but had not been achieved previously in Italian art. In the *Maestà* as well as in his other paintings and altarpieces, Duccio brought a narrative, human aspect to religious symbols by telling biblical stories in a sequence of pictures, a new approach in Italy that would become prevalent in centuries to follow.

A pupil of Duccio, Sienese painter Simone Martini (c. 1280–1344) inherited from his master many Gothic tendencies, such as the ability to bring human characteristics to the portrayal of religious scenes and figures. His altarpiece for the Siena Chapel, *Annunciation* (1333), humanizes Mary by giving her an

In a depiction of the Virgin receiving the angel's news similar to the altarpiece done for the Siena Chapel, Martini again seats the Virgin Mary in flowing robes in a throne-like chair with one hand drawn elegantly up to her face.

THE PAPAL SCHISM

The Papal Schism, also called the Great Schism of Western Christianity, was a split within the Catholic Church from 1378 to 1417, during which time two popes declared popedom, each with his own following. When Pope

Urban VI was elected in 1378, some cardinals—or church leaders—who were unhappy with Urban's leadership left Rome and established another **papacy** in Avignon in southern France. They elected a new pope, Clement VII, causing upheaval throughout Catholic Europe as countries had to decide which papacy to recognize and follow. The two papacies continued to function until 1417, when a council called for the resignation of both popes and elected a new pope in Rome, thus ending the schism.

expression of shock and fear as she recoils from the angel Gabriel and his announcement of the child she would bear. The figure of Mary—with her upraised right hand, curved form, and flowing robe—exudes the elegance common to Italian Gothic art. Martini went on to work for French kings in Naples and Sicily and eventually settled in Avignon in southern France. There, he came into contact with French painters, an experience that served to intensify the French Gothic characteristics of curved lines and realistic figures in his art, while also acquainting northern painters with the Italian style of his native region, which involved the use of rich, vibrant colors. The fusion of styles from various parts of Europe became known as International Gothic, and it spread across the continent in the early 14th century.

Just as the French Gothic style influenced Simone Martini, the Italian style influenced French artists such as Jean Pucelle (c. 1300–55), a pioneer of International Gothic in the illumination of manuscripts. A prolific artist, Pucelle traveled to Italy in the early 14th century. There, he viewed the works of Duccio and Martini, and upon his return to France, he infused the Italian influence into his own work by placing figures within actual physical and architectural settings, though his illuminations were still largely French Gothic in style, with naturally posed figures and decorative borders. Pucelle often used a technique known as grisaille, which involved painting in shades of gray with only faint splashes of color, and he was one of the first artists to use drolleries—marginal designs that commented on the text of a book. One of his most celebrated works, *Book of Hours of Jeanne d'Evreux* (c. 1325–28), a private prayer book for Queen Jeanne of France, used drolleries to illustrate religious scenes and to urge the reader to interact with the text.

Spanish altarpieces were made in the *retablo* style. Using an immense wooden framework, the painted narrative scenes (such as *Mounted Soldiers*, from Luis Borrassá's *Virgin and St. George*) covered the entire wall behind a church's altar.

Another important contributor to the International Gothic style was Luis Borrassá (1360–1426), a painter from a long line of Spanish artists. Early in his career, Borrassá painted for the royalty of Aragón in northeastern Spain, but around the year 1380, he set up his own workshop in Barcelona. In his altarpiece *Virgin and Saint George* (1399), made for the Church of San Francisco in a nearby town, Italian influence can be seen in the use of narrative scenes and the handling of space. Other aspects of the painting, such as the use of rich colors on a large, wall-sized wooden framework, show Borrassá's native Spanish influence, which helped to further develop the International Gothic style.

GOTHIC ART AND ARCHITECTURE

One of the most magnificent Gothic cathedrals is Notre-Dame de Paris. A famous symbol of the city, Notre-Dame stands on the Île de la Cité, an island in the Seine River in the heart of Paris. Begun in 1163 on the ideas of Bishop Maurice de Sully and completed in 1345, the architecture of Notre-Dame reflects many of the core elements of the French Gothic style. Flying buttresses support the height of the building, and stained-glass windows fill the interior with shimmering, changing colors, while individual panes illustrate biblical stories. At a length of 427 feet (130 m) and a height of 115 feet (35 m) to the

PLACE TO VISIT: CATHEDRAL OF NOTRE-DAME

Located on the Île de la Cité in the center of the city, Notre-Dame is one of the most visited sites in Paris. Considered one of the finest examples of Gothic architecture, Notre-Dame has withstood the raids of the French Revolution and the bombs of World War II. Visitors to the cathedral can view the towers and flying buttresses on

the exterior of the building, and once inside, they can gaze at the stained-glass rose windows; admire famous Gothic statues such as the *Virgin of Paris*, sculpted in the early 14th century by an unknown artist; and view the many small chapels that radiate from the main body of the church.

vaults, Notre-Dame is larger than other Gothic cathedrals, but even at its size, all of the details of the interior and exterior, including the two large towers and three portals on the western side and the stained-glass rose windows throughout the building, have been integrated to create a unified whole.

The rose window of Notre-Dame's north wall is one of its most beautiful and extraordinary architectural treasures. Designed by master builder Jean de Chelles (c. 1200–65) around the years 1250 to 1260, the circular stained-glass window is 43 feet (13 m) in diameter, covering a large expanse of the wall, and is held in place by only a thin **armature** of stone. The paring down of the supportive stone structure was a bold and innovative way to let in as much light as possible, spurred by Gothic enthusiasm for light and its attributes. A majority of the original stained glass of the north window is still intact after hundreds of years, and in its panes, Old Testament stories whirl around the Virgin Mary at the center. The color of the window is primarily blue, suggesting the northern sky beyond as well as the heavens.

In the small village of Chartres, southwest of Paris, another Gothic cathedral rises to magnificence. The Chartres Cathedral, built from 1194 to 1260, brings together the hallmarks of Gothic structure such as ribbed vaulting, the pointed arch, and flying buttresses. After fires in 1134 and 1194 destroyed the city's original Romanesque cathedral, the rebuilding of the Chartres Cathedral began. The work was costly, and many church officials gave all or most of their incomes to support the construction. When funding grew tight in the 1220s, officials raised taxes, causing riots among the townspeople. Even amidst such turmoil, the cathedral emerged as a masterpiece of Gothic architecture, inspiring awe in all who gazed upon it.

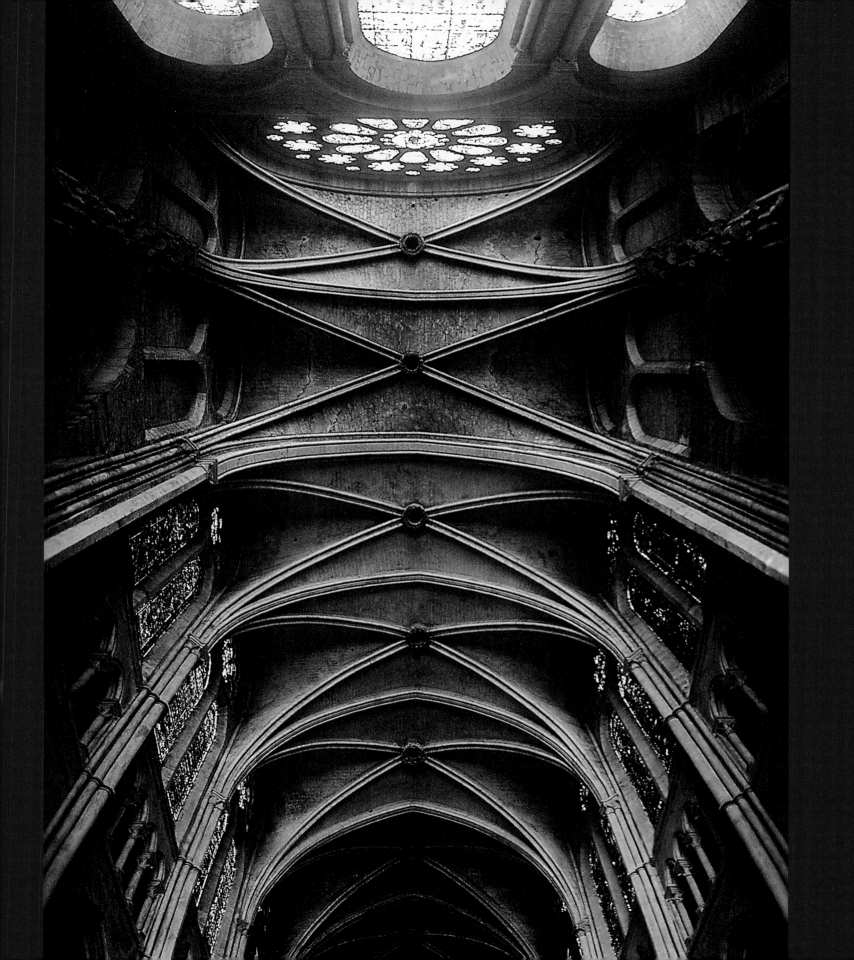

The real-life Ekkehard and Uta were ancestors of the bishop who commissioned their sculptures, Dietrich II, a member of the ruling family of Naumburg. Traces of pigment on the statues indicate that they had originally been painted.

One of the most moving and emotional devotional images to emerge during the Gothic period was the pietà. A pietà, which means "compassion" in Italian, is a figure, usually a small statue, of the Virgin Mary mourning over the dead body of her son, Jesus Christ. One of the earliest pietàs, the *Roettgen Pietà* (c. 1300), carved from wood by an unknown German sculptor, is among the most famous pietàs in the world due to the expressiveness of Mary's features and the ravaged body of Jesus. Mary looks down at Jesus's body with a hopeless, anguished expression; Jesus's body is shrunken and lifeless, and large drops of blood trickle from his wounds. The purpose of the pietà is to arouse compassion and meditation, and the *Roettgen Pietà* evokes a sense of shared pain and suffering in its viewers.

Even as the pietà became more common, secular art was also being incorporated into churches. *Ekkehard and Uta* (c. 1245–60), two statues in the Naumburg Cathedral in eastern Germany, reflect Gothic humanism and the introduction of nonreligious art into the cathedral. In the 11th century, Ekkehard of Meissen and his Polish wife Uta had given money to aid in the building of the Naumburg Cathedral. By the time the statues were sculpted in the 13th century by an unknown artist, Ekkehard and Uta had long been dead, but the statues of the two are extraordinarily lifelike and distinct, revealing the great skill of the sculptor in using live models as well as his imagination and reflecting the naturalism of the Gothic period. The **aristocracy** of the couple is captured in Ekkehard's warrior-like pose and Uta's elegant gesture of drawing her cloak to her cheek. *Ekkehard and Uta*, along with 10 other statues of benefactors, were placed on pedestals inside the chapel at window-level, a height usually reserved for saints and prophets.

In the famine-afflicted, warring times of 14th-century Germany, representations of the physical suffering of Mary, such as the *Roettgen Pietà*, helped people identify with a religious figure on a personal level. The Germanic term for such an image of Mary mourning her son was *vesperbild*, later to be popularized in Italian as *pietà*.

PLACE TO VISIT: NATIONAL LIBRARY OF THE NETHERLANDS

The National Library of the Netherlands in The Hague, Netherlands, hosts a large collection of illuminated manuscripts. More than 400 medieval manuscripts containing 11,000 illustrations, some of which date back to the year A.D. 900, are displayed in the library. The collection ranges from a

fragment of a manuscript to an extensive book in several parts. Among the manuscripts visitors can view are *The Book of Hours of Simon de Varie*, illustrated by French artist Jean Fouquet in 1455, and *The Book of Hours of Isabella of Castile* (c. 1390), illustrated by an unknown master in Milan, Italy.

Although secular pieces such as *Ekkehard and Uta* had begun to appear in cathedrals, religious art was still prevalent. Nicola Pisano's pulpit at the Pisa Baptistery in Pisa, Italy, represents the Gothic focus on narration in art. By the time the pulpit was built in 1260, the Franciscan sect of the Catholic Church had started to use more images in its works and sermons, and Pisano's job was to create a pulpit that illustrated the Word of God through pictures. The sculptures on the upper part of the six-sided, open pulpit illustrate biblical scenes, such as the Annunciation and Nativity. The human emotions of adoration and wonder are evident in the expressions of the figures, another Gothic feature of this finely detailed sculpture.

The frescoes of Giotto di Bondone (1267–1337) in the Arena Chapel in Padua, Italy, are among the most splendid frescoes in the world. Painted in 1305–06 on the walls of the Arena Chapel, a private chapel named after a nearby ancient Roman arena, the frescoes are arranged in three tiers of narrative scenes that focus on events from the lives of the Virgin and of Christ. The 38 scenes are set at the height of drama and feeling. In the fresco *The Lamentation*, Giotto depicts the death of Jesus Christ, but the sorrow of the scene is not confined to the Virgin Mary; John the Baptist flings his arms in despair, and angels hover above the mourners with grief upon their faces, evoking an emotional response in viewers. Such an emotional relationship between spectators and a work of art was innovative and exciting, and many artists after Giotto employed similar emotive techniques. Giotto's narrative scheme would also influence later Renaissance artists for whom the painted chapel was an important type of art.

Giotto di Bondone set himself apart from his contemporaries by daring to depict fully emotive, three-dimensional figures in his narrative frescoes instead of using symbols to create highly stylized characters.

While Giotto's frescoes in the Arena Chapel (opposite) strove to tell the story of Jesus' life using narrative scenes, Ambrogio Lorenzetti's sweeping frescoes portrayed abstract principles of good and bad governance, such as *Detail of Justice Inspired by Wisdom* (left), from *Allegory of Good Government*.

Another important set of frescoes in Italian Gothic was Ambrogio Lorenzetti's (c. 1290–1348) *Allegory* (1338–40) sequence in the Siena City Hall in Siena, Italy. Lorenzetti's frescoes are secular rather than religious in nature and provide a portrait of medieval Siena and its surrounding countryside. The frescoes contrast the effects of good government with the effects of bad government, an idea influenced by the turbulent, corrupt politics and power struggles of the time. In one fresco, *An Allegory of Good Government in the City*, Lorenzetti painted a panorama of Siena—complete with palaces, markets, churches, and towers—in which tradesmen perform their crafts and maidens dance. In *An Allegory of Good Government in the Country*, peasants work the fields, and the mountains of Tuscany rise in the distance. In contrast, *An Allegory of Bad Government in the Country* shows a dry, desolate countryside beneath a dark sky, battered houses, and toiling peasants. One of Lorenzetti's great achievements in the *Allegory* frescoes was his creation of a natural scale of human figures in their environment, showing the increasing knowledge of perspective among Gothic artists.

Although it started in France, the Flamboyant style soon reached Italy and influenced the design of many cathedrals there, such as the one in Milan, which showcases the characteristically lacy, ornamental stonework on every feature, including its windows.

LATE GOTHIC AND THE RENAISSANCE

The Gothic period spanned more than 200 years and saw many variations and evolutions in style and technique. As the Gothic period progressed into the Late Gothic period around the turn of the 15th century, the decoration of cathedrals grew more intricate and elegant, and the buildings soared to loftier heights. In France, much Late Gothic architecture of the early 15th century was created in the Flamboyant style, characterized by the flamelike, ornamental decoration of windows. The move toward more decorative elements in architecture was due in part to an increased appreciation of beauty. Another influence on the move of art to the ornamental was the growing materialism among citizens and royalty. Gothic architecture was no longer reserved only for cathedrals but was also used for the castles and houses of the wealthy. Many castles and mansions built during the Gothic period boasted towering spires and stained-glass windows.

During the 14th century, the S-curve emerged as a structural device that became inherent to the Gothic figure and evoked a sense of naturalness in the figure's stance. In earlier statues and sculptures, the figure was often depicted as standing straight and upright. Use of the Gothic S-curve, however, lent

Overcrowded and located on a major trade route (the Danube River), the city of Vienna, Austria, was disastrously susceptible to the Black Death. Another strain of bubonic plague beset the city in 1679, after which the ornate Plague Column was built as a memorial.

Prospectus Columnæ S. Sanct. Trinitatis ex voto avetendam Anno 1679. hîc Viennæ sævientem pestem ab Augustissimo Piæ memoriæ Leopoldo I. in perpetuam rei memoriam ædificatæ vulgò auf dem Graben.

Prospect der H. Dreyfaltigkeits-Saülen auf dem Graben, so als ey der A° 1679. allhier grassierenden Pest von Ihro Kayserl. Majesti glorwürdigster Gedächtnis zum ewigen Angedencken erbauet

Sal. Kleiner I. E. M. del.

Cum Priv. Sac. Cæs. Maj.

a bend to the body, so that a slightly curved "S" could be drawn down the middle of the figure. The use of the S-curve marked a trend toward accurate, natural human depiction that quickened in the Late Gothic period.

As these new developments in Gothic art were occurring, widespread changes were also taking place in society. Feudalism began to decline in the 14th century as stronger, more centralized governments, such as the Italian **city-states**, came into power. Increased exploration and trade with the distant world brought riches to Europe, and **economic** pursuit and curiosity about unexplored territories began to replace religious fervor. Heightened prosperity among the citizens of Europe, especially in Italy, caused a resurgence of interest in painting. The frescoes of Duccio and Giotto were revered, and the artists themselves were respected. Ambrogio Lorenzetti's *Allegory* frescoes depict the Sienese city-state at the pinnacle of its glory.

Just a few years after the *Allegory* frescoes were painted, Europe was stricken with the devastating **plague** known as the Black Death, an epidemic spread by both flea-infested rats and airborne bacteria. The Black Death reached Italy in 1348 and swept across the rest of the continent at a shocking pace: by 1390, it had killed more than one-third of Europe's population, including Lorenzetti and other artists. With the plague's destruction at its peak, Gothic artist Francesco Traini (c. 1310–63) painted the fresco *The Triumph of Death* (c. 1350–52) on a funerary structure near the Pisa Cathedral. The painting depicts the living pursued by the warriors of death, a **theme** that reflects the horrors of plague-wracked Europe.

After the devastation of the Black Death in the late 14th and early 15th centuries, artists looked to make sense of the world. Emphasis turned away

THE CATHOLIC CHURCH AND FEUDALISM

The Roman Catholic Church was the only Christian church in Europe during the Middle Ages, and because of Christianity's widespread popularity in Europe, the Church was a powerful force. Church leaders such as bishops and archbishops often held high positions in government and in the king's council. Because of their

role as both government and spiritual leaders, bishops had a say in many of the laws that were passed, including those that imposed taxes upon the people. The tax money was often used for cathedral building, but sometimes wealth led to corruption in the Church, and some leaders kept the money for themselves. Village priests, on the other hand, were usually not as wealthy as the bishops and often tended the sick and taught villagers to read.

The period known as the Renaissance began in Italy, where its influence can be seen in such cities as Venice (above). Venice was an important gathering place for Renaissance scholars who studied ancient Greek texts and culture.

from the spiritual and toward ideas of the natural world and human life. Accurate depiction of humans and their surroundings, which had begun in the Gothic period, evolved into the representational, lifelike art of the Renaissance. Beginning with Italian painters such as Duccio, faces and bodies became more pronounced and realistic. The architectural structures that had served merely as frames surrounding the figures during the Gothic period developed into important aspects of the paintings themselves.

Along with an increased desire for naturalism, an increased sense of individualism spread throughout Europe. During the Gothic period, many

people had thought that the sole purpose of human life was to secure everlasting spiritual salvation, but during the Renaissance, the idea that humans had a moral purpose on Earth, aside from a religious one, prevailed. This idea, along with the growing sense that one is in control of one's destiny, led to a strong awareness of self among the citizens of Europe, and painted portraits were in high demand among the royal and wealthy. From these new ideas about humanity and individuality, the modern age sprang.

For centuries, many scholars and historians viewed the Middle Ages as a dark and empty period that separated the glorious years of Roman

The legends of King Arthur and his Knights of the Round Table are some of the best-known medieval tales from Great Britain. During the Renaissance, it was asserted that the legends were based on historical fact, but a debate has gone on for centuries.

Classicism from the Renaissance. In the late 18th and early 19th centuries, however, renewed interest in the Middle Ages and Gothic art sprang up. Because the medieval period is considered an age of faith, many artists of the 19th century viewed Gothic art as representative of the pure spirituality that had been replaced by scientific reason in the 17th and 18th centuries. Art of the Romantic movement in the 19th century returned to medieval subjects and focused on evoking emotional responses in its spectators. Communication between a work of art and a spectator had been a novel idea during the Gothic period, but it was the cornerstone upon which much subsequent art, including Romantic art, was built. In addition to the Romantic movement, other movements, such as the Expressionist movement in the late 19th and early 20th centuries, dwelt on bringing forth feelings in their viewers. Today, evoking emotion is the basis of much contemporary art.

Emotion was not the only lasting influence of Gothic art, however; Gothic subject matter also played a role in subsequent art styles. One offshoot of the Romantic movement, Pre-Raphaelitism, focused on using medieval techniques as well as subjects, such as King Arthur and the idea of courtly love. Religious subject matter in art has also remained prevalent throughout the centuries.

No other artistic style had as much impact on subsequent architecture as did the Gothic style. Even long after the great age of cathedral building ended due to war, plague, and shifts in governmental power, Gothic cathedrals continued to influence architects and builders. In England, the tendency toward using Gothic elements in architecture never fully ended, and Gothic characteristics appeared in various structures such as Oxford's

The Smithsonian Institution Building, known as the Castle, was designed by James Renwick

to house all of the Institution's museums, lecture halls, and laboratories. The chapel-like west wing (farthest to the right, above), which featured vaulted ceilings characteristic of the Gothic style, originally held the Institution's library collection.

Tom Tower, built in 1681, and Westminster Abbey's western towers, built in 1722 and 1745. Because the Gothic style called to mind the age of faith and spirituality, Gothic elements were especially popular in the construction of churches and cathedrals. In the late 18th century, a full-fledged Gothic revival blossomed in England with the building of Strawberry Hill, the mansion of writer and architect Sir Horace Walpole, in 1749. Walpole's mansion, complete with turrets and battlements, evokes the romance reminiscent of the medieval age. Coinciding with the Romantic movement, the Gothic revival spread from England to other parts of Europe and the United States. The Smithsonian Institution in Washington, D.C., built between 1848 and 1855, reflects Gothic tendencies in its red sandstone towers and chimneys that reach toward the clouds.

Created during a time of plague and famine, war and ardent faith, Gothic art has endured through the centuries to depict the life and ideas of the Middle Ages. Sprawling cathedrals represent the dedication of the architects and builders of the time, and altarpieces, statues, frescoes, and tapestries illustrate the spirituality of medieval people. Today, thousands of people from all over the world travel to Europe to visit Gothic cathedrals, a testament to the fact that Gothic art still has the power to awe and astonish as it did more than 800 years ago.

TIMELINE

1095	The First Crusade begins
1130s	Abbot Suger begins to build the church of Saint-Denis
1163	Construction begins on the Notre-Dame Cathedral in Paris
1215	The Magna Carta limits the power of English kings
1220	Construction begins on Salisbury Cathedral in England
1226	Francis of Assisi, patron saint of animals and the environment, dies
1271	Explorer Marco Polo of Venice journeys to China
1291	The Crusades end
1305	Giotto di Bondone begins painting the frescoes of the Arena Chapel
1308	Italian poet Dante Alighieri begins writing *The Divine Comedy*
1311	Duccio di Buoninsegna paints the *Maestà Altarpiece* for the Siena Cathedral
1326	The cannon is used in battle for the first time
1337	The Hundred Years' War between France and England begins
1348	The Black Death reaches Italy
1350	The Flamboyant style emerges
1378	Theologian John Wycliffe begins translating the Bible into English
1387	English poet Geoffrey Chaucer begins *The Canterbury Tales*
1399	Luis Borrassá paints *Virgin and Saint George*
1400	The spread of the Black Death slows
1424	Italian artists Masolino and Masaccio begin the Brancacci Chapel frescoes, considered the beginning of the Italian Renaissance

GLOSSARY

anonymous	a person whose name or identity is not known
aristocracy	the group of people of the highest social rank, often the wealthy or descendents of royalty
armature	a skeletal framework built as a support
Byzantine Empire	a Greek-speaking Roman empire that was centered in present-day Istanbul during the 4th through the 15th centuries
city-states	regions controlled completely by a central city
economic	having to do with the way money, goods, and services affect a society
famine	extreme scarcity of food among a population or group

flying buttresses	freestanding stone supports that arch away from the structure they are supporting
frescoes	paintings made on walls or ceilings
Islamic	pertaining to the religion of Islam, which holds that Allah is God and follows the teachings of his prophet, Muhammad
medieval	having to do with the Middle Ages, a period in Europe between A.D. 500 and 1450
papacy	the office and jurisdiction of a pope
parchment	heavy, paper-like material made from sheepskin or goatskin
peasants	people who own or work on small farms
philosophers	people who study ideas such as truth, wisdom, the nature of reality, and knowledge
plague	any serious disease that spreads quickly to many people and causes death
Romanesque	the style of architecture that prevailed in Europe from the 9th through the 12th centuries and was characterized by thick walls and narrow windows
silhouettes	dark outlines seen against a light background
symbols	designs or objects that represent something else
tapestries	heavy pieces of cloth with pictures or patterns woven into them
theme	the main subject or idea of a piece of art

BIBLIOGRAPHY

Aubert, Marcel. *The Art of the High Gothic Era.* New York: Greystone Press, 1966.

Cole, Bruce, and Adelheid Gealt. *Art of the Western World: From Ancient Greece to Post-Modernism.* New York: Simon & Schuster, 1989.

Deuchler, Florence. *Gothic Art.* New York: Universe Books, 1973.

Focillon, Henri. *The Art of the West in the Middle Ages.* Volume II. London: Phaidon Press, 1963.

Gardner, Louise. *Art through the Ages.* Orlando, Fla.: Harcourt Brace, 1991.

Janson, H. W., and Anthony F. Janson. *History of Art.* 6th Edition. New York: Harry N. Abrams, 2001.

Tolman, Rolf, ed. *The Art of Gothic: Architecture, Sculpture, Painting.* Cologne, Germany: Konemann Verlagsgesellschaft mbH, 1998.

Zarnecki, George. *Art of the Medieval World.* Englewood Cliffs, N.J.: Prentice-Hall, 1975.

INDEX